Contents

Why do bugs build?

Most **bugs** build homes to protect themselves and their young from enemies and the weather. Some bugs build to store food, others build to catch food.

Some African **termites** build towers as tall as giraffes!

Termites are the best bug builders. Their towers are often taller than people!

Bug Zone

Bugs that

Build

Barbara Taylor

Chrysalis Children's Books

First published in the UK in 2003 by
Chrysalis Children's Books
An imprint of Chrysalis Books Group Plc
The Chrysalis Building, Bramley Road, London W10 6SP

Paperback edition first published in 2005

Copyright © Chrysalis Books Group Plc 2003
Text by Barbara Taylor

ISBN 1 84138 818 8 (hb)
ISBN 1 84458 267 1 (pb)

British Library Cataloguing in Publication Data
for this book is available from the British Library.

Editorial manager: Joyce Bentley
Assistant editor: Clare Chambers

Project manager and editor: Penny Worms
Designer: Angie Allison
Picture researcher: Jenny Barlow
Consultant: Michael Chinery

Printed in China
10 9 8 7 6 5 4 3 2 1

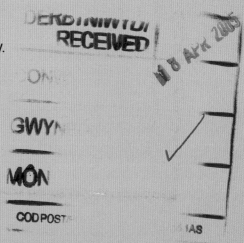

Words in bold can be found in the glossary on page 30.

All reasonable efforts have been made to trace the relevant copyright holders of the images contained within
this book. If we were unable to reach you, please contact Chrysalis Education.

B = bottom; C = centre; L = left; R = right; T = top.
Front Cover Montage (main) RSPCA Photolibrary/Wild Images/Carol Buchanan BL FLPA/Panda/A. Barghi BCL
FLPA/B. Casals BCR RSPCA Photolibrary/Geoff du Feu BR FLPA/Minden Pictures/M. Moffett Back Cover L
Papilio/Bjorn Backe R Warren Photographic/Kim Taylor 1 (see cover) 4 FLPA/M. Newman 5 T FLPA/G. E Hyde B
SPL/ E. R Degginger 6 RSPCA Photolibrary/Wild Images/John Downer 7 T RSPCA Photolibrary/Les Borg B
FLPA/B. Casals 8 RSPCA Photolibrary/Wild Images/Andrew Mounter 9 Ecoscene/Wayne Lawler 10
OSF/Frank Schneidermeyer 11 Ecoscene/Peter Currell 12 T FLPA/A. Visage B RSPCA Photolibrary/Wild I
images/Martin Dohrn 13 Papilio/Robert Pickett 14 M & P Fogden 15 T Papilio/Ken Wilson B FLPA/B.
Casals 16 Papilio/Michael Maconachie 17 Papilio/Ken Wilson 18 FLPA/S. Maslowski 19 T
FLPA/Minden Pictures/M. Moffett B Corbis/ Michael Busselle 20 (see cover) 21 FLPA/B. Casals 22
(see cover) 23 T Ecoscene/Kjell Sandved B Ecoscene/Chinch Gryniewicz 24 FLPA/A. Visage
25 T FLPA/B. Casals B RSPCA Photolibrary/Wild Images/Scott McKinley 26 Papilio/Rob
Pickett 27 FLPA/G. E Hyde 28 Papilio/Laura Sivell 29 M & P Fogden.

A **bumblebee's** untidy nest is a nursery for young bees and a food store.

Many bug builders are **social** bugs, living in big groups. Others are **solitary** bugs, living on their own.

Many **spiders** build silk webs to catch flying **insects**.

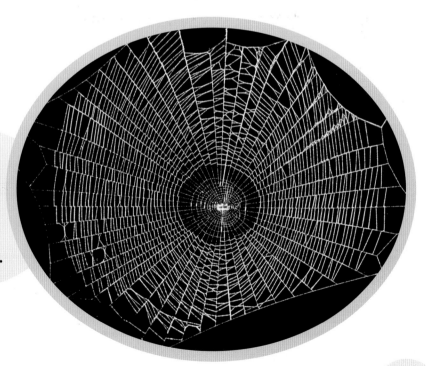

What do bugs build with?

Some **wasps** scrape off pieces of wood and mix it with their own **spit** to make paper nests.

Some bugs use natural materials for building, such as leaves, sticks, wood and mud.

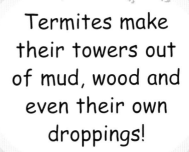

Termites make their towers out of mud, wood and even their own droppings!

Other bugs make their building materials inside their own bodies, such as **silk** and **wax**.

You can see the thread of silk coming out of the back end of this spider.

Honeybees build their homes using flakes of wax made in the back part of their bodies.

Leaf weavers

Some **ants** build nests out of living leaves. The ants hold onto each other in teams and pull the leaves together.

One, two, three. . .PULL! One ant working on its own would not be big enough or strong enough to pull these leaves together.

You can see the white silk holding the leaves together in this nest of green tree ants.

The ants glue the leaves together using the sticky silk made by their own young, called ant **larvae**.

Colonies of African weaver ants build their leafy nests together – there may be up to 150 nests in 20 neighbouring trees.

Diggers and carpenters

Carpenter ants build their nests by tunnelling into wood using their jaws.

Not all ants make their nests out of leaves. Many of them dig nests in the soil, or inside the branches, trunks or roots of trees.

Wood ants live in huge colonies. One nest contains up to 500,000 ants and may cover an area the size of a tennis court under the ground.

The Texas shed-builder ant makes little 'sheds' out of chewed-up plants. Inside, it keeps greenfly so it can drink the sweet honeydew they make. It's rather like people keeping cows for their milk!

Wood ants protect their underground nest with a mound of soil, twigs and pine needles.

Mud skyscrapers

Termites are the master builders of the bug world. For their size, they build the largest structures of all living creatures. The tall towers help to keep their underground nests cool.

The 'umbrella' on top of this termite mound helps to keep off the rain.

Underground, the termites raise their young and may also grow food.

Some termites build tree-top nests like this one. Both types of termite nest have walls as hard as rock.

Termite nests on the ground are built of mud or sand. Tree nests are usually made from wood fibres mixed with termite spit.

Some termite towers are 1000 times the height of their builders!

Paper nests

A large wasp's nest can contain over 10,000 wasps.

Some wasps live in large paper nests, which they make from chewed wood mixed with spit. They build layers of neat cells, which contain eggs or baby wasps.

Wasps always build six-sided cells. This is because it is the best shape for fitting many cells together.

In cool countries, the wasps cover their nest with layers of wasp paper. This helps to keep the nest warm.

The queen glues her eggs into the cells to stop them falling out.

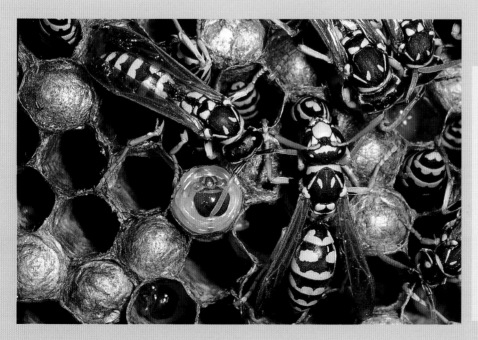

Unlike bees, wasps do not store food in their cells. They only use them as homes for their young.

Home alone

Many types of wasp live on their own and build little homes for their young. Inside, they leave food, so when the young wasps hatch out of the eggs, they can feed themselves.

Potter wasps build homes for their young out of mud, making a little 'pot'.

These digger wasps are fully grown and ready to come out of their wooden tunnels.

Some solitary wasps make their nests inside plants, in the ground or in rotten wood. Others build nests on rocks, trees or leaves.

Plasterer bees line their nests with dried spit. It forms a smooth plaster, just as people use plaster on the walls of their homes.

17

Hard-working bees

This wild honeybee nest has been built inside a hollow tree trunk.

Wild honeybees build nests in tree holes, roof spaces or caves. A big nest may contain over 60,000 bees. They make the nest from wax that they produce themselves.

Next time you have honey for breakfast remember that bees make honey from flower nectar mixed with their own spit!

The wax cells in a beehive are for storing honey and **pollen**, and are homes for the eggs and young. The adults feed the pollen and honey to the young bees.

People build **hives** for bees to nest in. They can then scrape off the wax and drain the honey to sell.

In cool countries, honeybees survive the cold winter, when there are no flowers to feed from, by eating the **honey** they make.

Bee loners

This leaf-cutter bee is carrying a piece of leaf to make a little home for her young.

Female leaf-cutter bees make their nests on their own. They snip off bits of leaf with their scissor-like jaws. Then they make little parcels, gluing the leaves together with spit and leaf sap.

20

Inside the parcel, the bee puts a mixture of yellow pollen and honey, plus a single egg. She then seals it up with more pieces of leaf and flies away.

A leaf-cutter bee can cut pieces of leaf from plants in only about three seconds.

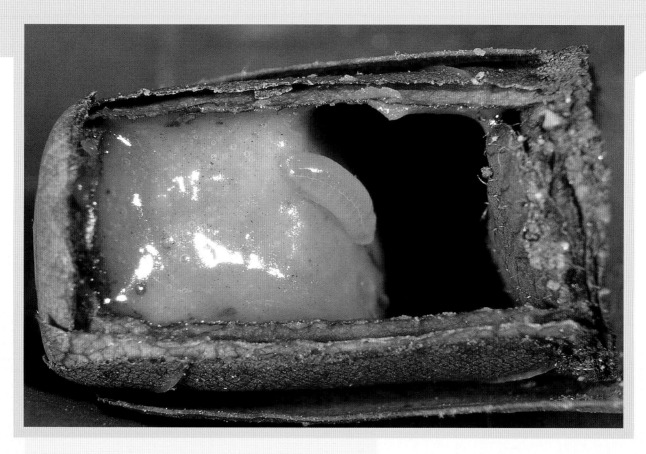

When the egg hatches, the larva eats the pollen and honey.

Silk shelters

Many spiders build silk nests to live in or to protect their young, not for catching **prey**.

The largest spider cities may be home to up to 20,000 spiders.

This funnel-weaver spider is waiting at the 'front door' of its home, hoping to grab passing prey.

A huge spider city like this may be home to hundreds or even thousands of spiders. Only about 30 kinds of spider live and build in groups.

Spiders that nest together in giant webs may hunt over the web in **packs**. They can catch much larger prey than if they hunted alone.

The female nursery-web spider builds a silk tent to protect her babies.

Building burrows

The front legs of the mole cricket are like shovels, perfect for scooping up soil – just like a real mole's.

Two of the best diggers in the bug world are mole crickets and sand wasps. Male mole crickets sit at the mouths of their burrows and make purring sounds to attract mates.

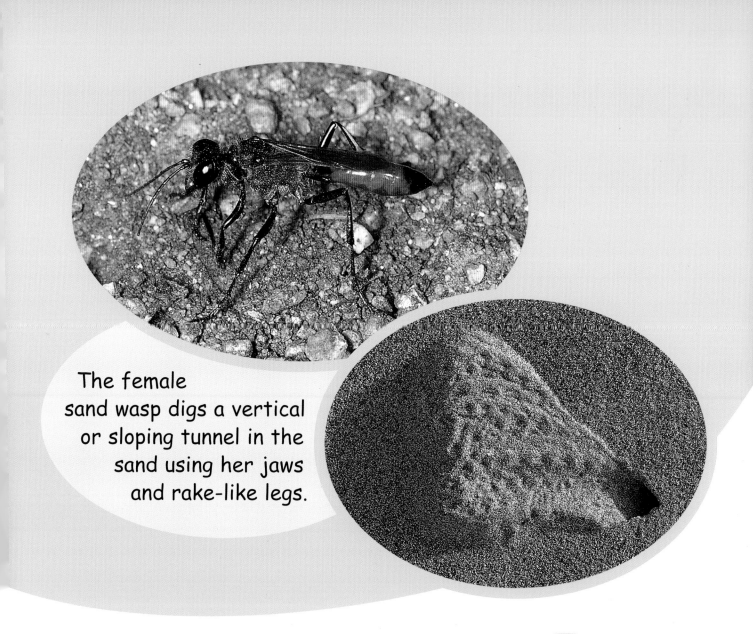

The female sand wasp digs a vertical or sloping tunnel in the sand using her jaws and rake-like legs.

Sand wasps build burrows for their young. They put food and an egg inside, then seal up the entrance with sand or a stone.

The funnel-shaped entrance to a mole cricket's burrow makes his calls louder – like a megaphone.

Mobile homes and changing rooms

Most caddis fly larvae spin sticky silk thread around their bodies, to which they stick sand, shells, leaves or twigs. They carry this 'house' around with them.

Some young bugs build cases around themselves to give them **camouflage** and protection from enemies.

Often these body suits are built from materials made by the young themselves when they are ready to change into adults.

The **cocoon** of a silk moth is made from one very long silk thread more than 800 metres long.

The silk moth caterpillar builds a cocoon of silk around itself before changing into an adult moth.

Plant partners

Some bugs use plants to build homes for them. They lay eggs on the plants, and the feeding larvae cause such irritation that the plant grows a **gall** over them.

Underneath an oak leaf, you might find these spangle galls. Each contains a tiny wasp larva.

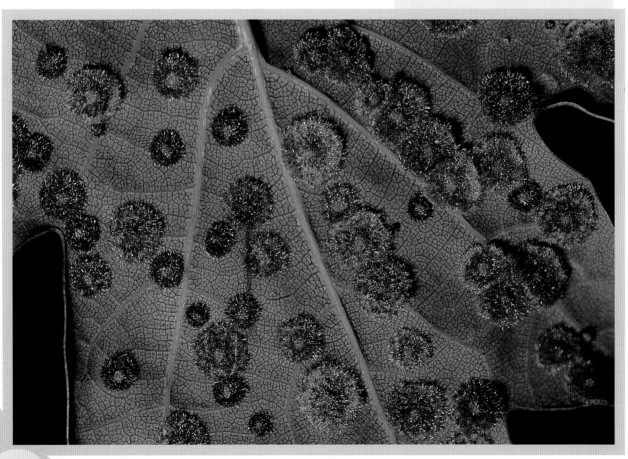

Armies of ants live inside the large thorns of a bull's horn acacia tree. The ants drill a hole in the thorn and then make their home in the hollow inside.

Many ants make their homes inside the stems or thorns of plants. The plants and the ants seem to help each other to survive.

In return for food and protection, some ants defend their plant homes against bugs that may harm them.

Words to remember

ant A small insect that lives with other ants in a large group called a colony.

bug A true bug is a type of insect with a stabbing beak. The word 'bug' is now used to mean any type of minibeast.

bumblebee A furry insect with a deep buzz and often with black and yellow stripes. Most bumblebees are larger than honeybees.

camouflage Colours or patterns that blend in with the background.

cocoon A silk case spun by some young insects before turning into adults.

colony A group of animals of the same kind that live closely together.

gall An abnormal plant growth caused by young insects or other tiny creatures living inside the plant.

hive A hollow box made by people for bees to live in.

honey A sweet, yellow liquid made by bees from flower nectar and saliva (spit).

honeybee A slim, striped insect that often lives in hives made by people.

insect A minibeast with three parts to its body and six legs. Most insects can fly.

larva A young insect that looks different from its parents. A larva is usually the feeding and growing stage in the life cycle. The word for more than one larva is larvae.

pack A group of animals that hunts together.

pollen A yellow dust produced by flowers that is full of goodness. Some insects feed their young on pollen.

prey An animal that is killed or eaten by another animal.

silk A fine, strong fibre produced by spiders and some insects, which is used to make webs and cocoons.

social Living together. Social insects live and work together. All ants and termites, and some bees and wasps are social.

solitary Living alone.

spider A minibeast (not an insect) with eight legs, two parts to its body and two poisonous fangs.

spit A liquid called saliva, which is made in the mouth and starts to break down food.

termite A social insect with biting mouthparts, often without wings.

wasp A stinging insect related to bees and ants with two pairs of wings which hook together.

wax A soft, waterproof, yellow substance made by bees to build their nests.

Index